WHO DOES GOD SAY I AM?

DISCOVERING YOUR IDENTITY IN CHRIST

CATHERINE M. VITETTA

MANIFEST
PUBLICATIONS

ISBN: 978-1-951280-52-9

Unless otherwise noted, Scriptures are taken from the
KING JAMES VERSION®. Public Domain.

Other sources referenced include:
Clark's Bible Commentary, Vol 1, Public Domain;
Bridgeway Bible Commentary © Don Flemming 1988;
Believer's Bible Commentary ©Thomas Nelson 2016

Cover Design: Don Patton Creative,
Image credit: Freepik, Wirestock

DEDICATION & ACKNOWLEDGEMENTS

As always, all the praise, honor, glory, and gratitude goes to the originator of this book: the Holy Spirit of the living God! Truly, this book was His idea to begin with and completed only through His guidance.

I would like to give much thanks to my pastor, Dan Hudson, for his assistance in reviewing the content of this book to ensure scriptural correctness. Pastor Dan's friendship, mentorship, and leadership has been a huge blessing in my life for which I will be forever grateful to the Lord!

Finally, I want to thank Manifest International for their Christ-centered assistance and guidance in bringing this book, as well as my other books, to fruition.

To God be the glory!

CONTENTS

i   Introduction: 1
I am... loved

1   Chapter 1:   9
I am... a new creature in Christ

2   Chapter 2:   17
I am... a child of the living God

3   Chapter 3:   25
I am... redeemed and forgiven

4   Chapter 4:   35
I am... no longer a slave to sin

5   Chapter 5:   43
I have... eternal life with God

6   Chapter 6:   51
I was... created with a purpose

7   Chapter 7:   59
I am... chosen

8   Chapter 8:   67
I have... peace in Christ

9   Chapter 9:   75
I have... victory in Christ

10   Chapter 10:   83
I am... not alone

11   Chapter 11:   91
Summary

INTRODUCTION:
I AM... LOVED

First and foremost, when asking the question of who does God say that I am, we need to be clear on the identity of the god to which I am referring. I am referring to the one true living God, the God of Abraham, Isaac, and Jacob as well as His only begotten Son, Christ Jesus.

When we look at history begin to unfold in the book of Genesis, we read that God is an eternal being with no beginning and no end. God created everything in the universe, beginning with light. Lastly, God created man, male and female, to tend the garden of Eden upon the earth, to be fruitful and multiply, and to be in direct fellowship with God. God gave man only one rule to follow in the garden, which was to not eat of the fruit from the tree of the knowledge of good and evil (Genesis 2:17.) We all know the story: Adam and Eve disobeyed God and ate from that very tree of which they were warned by God not to do so. In the moment of that first disobedience to God, called sin, man died spiritually and was separated from direct fellowship with God. A holy God cannot dwell with sin! (See Psalm 5:4)

But thankfully, from the very beginning, God had a plan to reconcile His beloved, yet sinful, creation back to Himself.

~

> *John 3:16 - [Jesus speaking] "For God so loved the world, that He gave His only begotten Son, that whosoever believeth in Him should not perish, but have everlasting life."*

Christ Jesus was God enrobed in flesh in the person of Jesus of Nazareth. He left His heavenly throne to come to this earth to live the perfect life as man and to be that final and perfect sacrifice required for the forgiveness of mankind's sins. A sinless and perfect Christ Jesus died the horrific death on the cross that all of sinful mankind deserved. Three days later, He rose from the dead. He currently reigns in heaven, seated at the right hand of the Father. Christ Jesus' sacrifice on the cross has saved mankind from the bondages of sin with its resultant second death in eternal torment separated from our Creator. As Romans 6:23 states, "For the wages of sin is death; but the gift of God is eternal life through Jesus Christ our Lord."

But here's the "catch," we must **choose** to accept the light of salvation offered through the sacrifice of Christ Jesus on the cross in order to be saved and have eternal life with the Lord after our physical death upon the earth. This is called salvation by the grace of God through faith in His only begotten Son, Christ Jesus.

~

> *John 14:6 - "Jesus saith unto him, "I am the way, the truth, and the life: no man cometh unto the Father, but by Me."*

That says it very clearly. Salvation, including reconciliation back to fellowship with God and eternal life with Him as God originally intended when He created mankind is **only** available through faith in His only begotten Son, Christ Jesus.

~

> *John 15:13 – [Jesus speaking] "Greater love hath no man than*

this, that a man lay down his life for his friends."

Think about this: God left His throne in heaven to come to this earth and enrobe Himself in flesh in the person of Jesus of Nazareth, only to knowingly and intentionally die a horrific death through crucifixion so that the sins of mankind could be forgiven! Romans 5:8 reminds us, "But God commendeth His love for us, in that, while we were yet sinners, Christ died for us." Once we accept Christ Jesus as our Lord and Savior, our sins are forgiven, and we can now have restored fellowship with God! How amazing is that?!?

God became a man of flesh and gave His life so that sinful mankind could be forgiven, saved and have restored fellowship with the Father. It does not matter what you have done in your past, Christ Jesus died for **you** because He loves **you** that much as His creation! And if you were the only person on this planet, Christ Jesus would still have gone to the cross for **you** alone! This means that regardless of who you are or what you have done, every person on the planet can truthfully and confidently say: "I am… loved!"

As you read this book, I would ask that you keep in mind that this is **not** a book about positive affirmations of qualities that we can "wish" upon ourselves. Once we come to Christ Jesus and are saved, meaning filled with the Holy Spirit of the living God, the bible has so much more to say about who we are! In this book, we will take a scriptural look at what God has to say about His beloved creation when we choose the light of salvation through faith in Christ Jesus! It is about knowing who we are in Christ.

As we reflect, we need to remember that because God is eternal, He can see the end from the beginning. God's word states in Philippians 1:6 that, "Being confident in this very thing, that He which hath begun a good work in you will perform it until the day of Jesus Christ." Once we make Christ Jesus our Lord, it implies that we will be obedient to Him, His teachings, and the promptings of the Holy Spirit who now dwells within us. Our spiritual development becomes a joint venture with God at the wheel. His word promises to complete the good work in us which He started! God sees and knows who we **are** in Him from the very beginning.

Early in my walk with the Lord, I had a terrible habit of self-deprecating thoughts of which I was very unaware. One day, the Lord spoke to my spirit and said, "Cathy, are you telling me that I made a mistake in calling you? Are you saying I am wrong?" Ouch! I never thought of it that way! I not only had to repent, but I had to learn what it is that God says about me, and align my thoughts with His thoughts in order to be effective for God's kingdom purposes in my life.

I soon learned that I was actually agreeing with what the enemy, Satan, had to say about me. Remember, even if Satan is unable to get you to walk away from your faith in Christ Jesus, his secondary plan of attack is always to render you ineffective for God's kingdom purposes. It is almost impossible to be a warrior for Christ when you are plagued with thoughts such as, "I'm not this, I can't that, but I've done this."

Therefore, it is my hope and prayer that each reader come to truly know what it is that God has to say about those of you who have accepted Christ Jesus as your Lord and Savior. Trust me when I say that there is nothing better on this earth than being in God's will for your life!

~

We can begin this journey by saying with confidence out loud:

"I am… loved!"

NOTES ON:
I AM... LOVED!

NOTES ON:
I AM... LOVED!

CHAPTER 1
I AM... A NEW CREATURE IN CHRIST

> *Galatians 2:20 - "I am crucified with Christ: nevertheless I live; yet not I, but Christ liveth in me: and the life which I now live in the flesh I live by the faith of the Son of God, who loved me, and gave Himself for me."*

Paul is saying that, just as Christ was crucified and died for him, his previously sinful self was crucified and is now dead. Because Paul had been saved and filled with the Holy Spirit of the living God, God no longer saw him as a sinner because of Paul's faith in what Christ Jesus did for him on the cross.

Prior to coming to Christ, every person is

inherently self-centered and sinful because, whether we know it or not, we are in bondage to sin. When we come to faith in Christ Jesus and are saved, we trade our sinfulness for God's righteousness. We are now set free from the bondage of (or inability to resist) sin. As we follow the promptings of the Holy Spirit, we change from being self-centered to now being God-centered in our heart, thoughts and deeds.

~

> 2 Corinthians 3:18 - "But we all, with open face beholding as in a glass the glory of the Lord, are changed into the same image from glory to glory, even as by the Spirit of the Lord."

This scripture tells us that we will experience these changes in heart, thought, and deeds gradually over time, as we change "from glory to glory." As time goes on, we will think and behave more and more like our Lord Jesus as we cooperate with the promptings of the Holy Spirit who now dwells within us! What an incredible promise!

Please remember that God is an eternal being who knows the end from the beginning. Often times, it is difficult for us to see any changes in ourselves, particularly in the early days of our walk with the Lord. We must trust and have faith that our God is true to His word and **will** complete the good work in us He started, as Philippians 1:6 promises. Our job is to love the Lord God, trust Him, have faith in Him, and work cooperatively with His promptings. In time, we will see those changes… as will others who are around us.

Early in my walk with the Lord, I prayed and asked Him to please make the changes He needed to make in me quickly, preferably instantaneously. His reply to my spirit took me by surprise. The Lord said, "Cathy, if I were to fix everything in you that needed fixing all at once, you would be crushed under the weight of it." EEK! I certainly did not expect that response from the Lord. But what I did learn from this experience was to rejoice in those changes that I could see, while I learned to wait patiently while trusting God for the future changes to come.

~

> *Ecclesiastes 3:11 - "He hath made everything beautiful in its time: also He hath set the world in their heart, so that no man can find out the work that God maketh from the beginning to the end."*

We can count on the promises of God! Why

would God not allow us to see the end result of His work in us prior to achieving it as this scripture indicates? One reason might be that some of us, such as myself, would excitedly rush through the process to achieve the presumed end result. First of all, such a person would be out of God's perfect timing. Secondly, if we are out of God's timing, many of the collateral interim "mini-achievements" might be missed altogether. Or, perhaps, we might become discouraged or fearful at the enormity of the goals set forth for us by God and not even get started in our kingdom purpose for the Lord. Finally, I am guessing that God probably likes to pleasantly surprise and amaze us with the end result of the good works He accomplishes in us in His perfect timing!

~

2 Corinthians 5:17 - "Therefore if any man be in Christ, he is a new creature: old things are passed away; behold, all things are become new."

This states it very clearly. Once we are saved and infilled with the Holy Spirit of the living God, we are no longer the same as we once were but are now and henceforth a new creature in Christ! This reflects our new **position** in Christ. It often takes time and growth in our newfound faith before we can put all of this into daily **practice**. On that special day when we are finally with the Lord in eternity, our position and our practice will become one in the same. Thankfully, God sees the end from the beginning!

~

> *Ephesians 4:22-24 - "That ye put off concerning the former conversation the old man, which is corrupt according to the deceitful lusts; and be renewed in the spirit of your mind; and that ye put on the new man, which after God is created in righteousness and true holiness."*

The apostle Paul is saying that who we are prior to being saved is essentially evil, sinful, corrupt, and Godless. Once we are filled with the Holy Spirit of the living God, the previous inner man dies and a new, regenerated man emerges. The Spirit of God now leads our heart and mind in the ways of a holy and righteous God rather than the former ways of sinful man. These inward changes in our heart and mind lead to outward changes in words and deeds. Hence, we actually **are** new creatures in Christ from the onset of salvation! And in time, we will manifest these changes to those around us. My Pastor likes to describe this process as "our character needs to catch up with our calling!"

~

> Ezekiel 11:19-20 - "And I will give them one heart, and I will put a new spirit within you; and I will take the stoney heart out of their flesh, and will give them an heart of flesh; that they may walk in my statutes, and keep mine ordinances, and do them: and they shall be My people, and I will be their God."

What a lovely explanation of what happens under the New Testament covenant when we are filled with the Holy Spirit of the living God! We are given new, soft hearts that reflect the character of God and the Lord's will. We will see and feel things differently, which changes our thoughts, which changes our actions all to be more reflective of God in quality. What an incredible promise!

~

Having accepted Christ Jesus as my Lord and Savior, I can confidently say out loud:

"I am... a new, beautiful creature in Christ!"

NOTES ON:
I AM... A NEW CREATURE IN CHRIST!

NOTES ON:

I AM... A NEW CREATURE IN CHRIST!

CHAPTER 2
I AM... A CHILD OF THE LIVING GOD

> *Ephesians 1:5 - "Having predestin-*
> *ated us unto the adoption of*
> *children by Jesus Christ unto*
> *Himself, according to the good*
> *pleasure of His will."*

Remember that we are saved by the grace of God through faith in His only begotten Son, Christ Jesus. This scripture is telling us that **all** those who **choose** the light of salvation through faith in God's only begotten Son are automatically adopted into the family of God. Although God did not have to adopt those who are in Christ, God predetermined that **all** who choose faith in Christ Jesus and are saved **are** automatically adopted into the family of God. This is the good pleasure of His will that we are now members of

God's family!

~

> *John 1:12-13 - "But as many as received Him, to them He gave power to become the sons of God, even to them that believe on His name: which were born, not of blood, nor of the will of the flesh, nor of the will of man, but of God.*

This beautiful passage of scripture tells us just how simple it really is to become a child of the living God. Again, when we come to faith in Christ Jesus, we are saved by grace through our faith. After we admit our need for forgiveness and salvation, look to Jesus as our Lord and Savior, and ask the Holy Spirit into our heart, we are saved or "born again." This rebirth is not a physical rebirth, but a spiritual rebirth. We have just been reborn into the family of God, and scripture tells us that this is the **only** way to become a child of the living God!

~

> *Romans 8:14-17 - "For as many as are led by the Spirit of God, they are the sons of God. For ye have*

not received the spirit of bondage again to fear; but ye have received the Spirit of adoption, whereby we cry, Abba, Father. The Spirit itself beareth witness with our spirit, that we are children of God; And if children, then heirs; and joint-heirs with Christ; if so be that we suffer with Him, that we may be also glorified together."

When we claim Christ Jesus as our Lord and Savior and the Holy Spirit resides within us, the word **Lord** implies our ensuing obedience to Him and His promptings. Our obedience to the Lord is demonstrated by our changed attitudes, thoughts, words, and behaviors over time.

And because we are now a child of the living God in restored fellowship with the Father through Christ, we can not only come before the throne of grace but we can address God as "Abba." Abba is a term for Father denoting closeness and affection. It is actually translated as "Daddy" or "Papa." Imagine that! The one true living God is our Daddy now! And because He is now our Daddy, we have all the privileges and responsibilities of adult children of God.

~

Galatians 4:6-7 - "And because ye are sons, God hath sent forth the Spirit of His Son into your hearts, crying, Abba, Father. Wherefore thou art no more a servant, but a son; and if a son, then an heir of God through Christ."

Consider this: our ensuing obedience to the Lord is not forced upon us as if we were slaves. Our ensuing obedience is willingly given to our Abba, God the Father, out of our love and gratitude for all that He has done for us! John 14:15 [Jesus speaking] says, "If ye love me, keep my commandments." Our obedience to God is the evidence that we love Him and that we are truly a child of the living God with all its privileges and responsibilities!

~

2 Corinthians 6:17-18 - "Wherefore come out from among them, and be ye separate, saith the Lord, and touch not the unclean thing; and I will receive you, and will be a Father unto you, and ye shall be my sons and daughters, saith the Lord Almighty."

When we become a child of the living God, our Father in heaven calls us to abstain from and avoid all evil that is in this fallen world. It is very similar to what natural parents expect from their children on this earth. A good parent sets boundaries.

The Believer's Bible Commentary[1] says it this way:

> "The recompense for standing with Christ outside the camp of evil is to know fellowship with the Father in a new and more intimate way. It does not mean that we become sons and daughters by obedience to His word, but that we are manifestly His sons and daughters when we behave in this way, and we will experience the joys and delights of sonship in a way we never have before."

~

Having accepted Christ Jesus as my Lord and Savior, I can now confidently say out loud:

"I am... a child of the living God!"

---

[1] Believer's Bible Commentary, 2nd edition. P.1867

NOTES ON:
I AM... A CHILD OF THE LIVING GOD!

NOTES ON:

I AM... A CHILD OF THE LIVING GOD!

NOTES ON:
I AM... A CHILD OF THE LIVING GOD!

CHAPTER 3
I AM... REDEEMED AND FORGIVEN

Out in the world today, preachers are teaching and preaching so many various versions of the forgiveness of God. Sadly, many of these teachings and preachings are false because they are partially based on assumption as well as the opinions of man. This chapter will seek to take a look at what the Word of God in the scriptures has to say about the forgiveness of God.

~

> 1 John 1:8-9 - "If we say that we have no sin, we deceive ourselves, and the truth is not in us. If we confess our sins, He is faithful and just to forgive us our sins, and to cleanse us from all unrighteousness."

Since the fall of man in the garden of Eden, man lost the ability to directly fellowship with God due to his sin. This is because a holy God will not dwell in the presence of sin (Psalm 5:4.) But the moment we admit our need for a Savior and come to faith in Christ Jesus and His substitutionary work on the cross on our behalf, we can be reconciled back to God by His extravagant grace. But part of coming to Christ involves a sincere, humble admission that one is a sinner in need of the mercy and forgiveness that can only come through faith in Christ Jesus. When our hearts are grieved over our sinful and fleshly nature with its resultant evil deeds so that we humbly ask for forgiveness, the Lord is faithful to forgive us of our sins. This beautiful inner cleansing comes at the time of our initial conversion to Christ. We **can** be washed white as snow and have restored fellowship with God!

~

> *Romans 3:24-25 - "Being justified freely by His grace through the redemption that is in Christ Jesus: whom God hath set forth to be a propitiation through faith in His blood, to declare His righteousness for the remission of sins that are past, through the forbearance of God;"*

Ephesians 1:7 - "In Whom we have redemption through His blood, the forgiveness of sins, according to the riches of His grace."

Let's break these scriptures down into manage-able parts so that we might understand them in their entirety. What does being justified actually mean? By definition, it means we are declared righteous by God. However, we must understand that we are **only** declared righteous because of God's unmerited, or undeserved, favor and grace, and **not** because we, as imperfect human beings, "deserve" to be called righteous. Only God is righteous.

What does propitiation mean? Propitiation is the act of appeasement, or payment, to God for the regaining of favor. In the Old Testament, divine law dictated that there needed to be the spilling of blood for the forgiveness of sin. This is prescribed in the Law of God in the sacrifices of animals at the temple to atone for the sins of the Israelites. The Lord God spoke this to Moses in Leviticus 17:11 "For the life of the flesh is in the blood: and I have given it to you upon the altar to make an atonement for your souls: for it is the blood that maketh atonement for the soul." The word *atonement* means to satisfy someone for an offense committed. The sacrifices of animals to atone for the sins of the people only partially atoned for sin for a short period of time. In other words, this was an imperfect system for the forgiveness of sins that was a foreshadow of what was to come. Ultimately, what was needed was a perfect and final blood sacrifice for the forgiveness of the sin of man once and for all. Since there has never been a perfect human being, **only** God enrobed in flesh in the man of Christ Jesus could be that final once and for all perfect sacrifice to atone for the sin of man.

When we come to Christ, we are saved by the grace of God through faith in His only begotten son, Jesus, and what He accomplished on the cross for us. Christ Jesus paid the price for **all** the sins of mankind with His precious shed blood. When we come to faith in what Christ Jesus did on the cross on our behalf, we essentially trade our sinfulness for the righteousness of Christ. Justification is a gift from a gracious God to those who do not deserve it in and of themselves. We are redeemed, forgiven, and cleansed so that our fellowship with the Father can be restored by grace through faith! What an amazing gift for those who choose it!

But what happens to our state of initial judicial forgiveness once we, as imperfect human beings, inadvertently commit sin after our initial cleansing? The answer actually comes in two parts as we look at the judicial forgiveness of God verses the parental forgiveness of God. Judicial forgiveness is that initial cleansing from sin when we come to Christ Jesus and take on His righteousness. This is our justification. Judicial forgiveness with its resultant restored fellowship with the Father remains as long as we remain in Christ.

Parental forgiveness will be an ongoing need for the duration of our lives on earth for all of us in Christ who will inadvertently commit sin from time to time. Let's look at the following five passages of scripture together in order to more fully understand the parental forgiveness of God after we come to faith in Christ Jesus:

~

> *Luke 24:47 - [Jesus speaking] "And that repentance and remission of sins should be preached in His name among all nations, beginning at Jerusalem."*

> *Acts 3:19 - "Repent ye therefore, and be converted, that your sins may be blotted out, when the times of refreshing shall come from the presence of the Lord."*

Acts 17:30 - "And the times of this ignorance God winked at; but now commandeth all men every where to repent."

Proverbs 28:13 - "He that covereth his sins shall not prosper: but whoso confesseth and forsaketh them shall have mercy."

2 Chronicles 7:14 - "If my people, which are called by my name, shall humble themselves, and pray, and seek my face, and turn from their wicked ways; then will I hear from heaven, and will forgive their sin, and will heal their land."

Did you notice a common theme among all five of these passages of scripture? It is crucial that we have a clear understanding of the parental forgiveness of God after we come to faith in Christ. Each of these passages talks about the **need** for repentance. But what is repentance? Webster's dictionary defines repentance as:

1. To turn from sin and dedicate oneself to the amendment of one's life
2. To feel regret or contrition; to change one's mind

Repentance is so much more than an empty

apology. It means that we feel remorse about the sin in our lives. We now purpose to align our thoughts about the sin with the thoughts of God. We will ultimately turn away from the sin and **stop** sinning! How can a Holy God forgive us our sins if we feel no remorse and have no intention of stopping from participation in that sin? If this were the case and sin were forgiven automatically whether we stop doing it or not, there would have been no need for Christ Jesus to go to the cross.

When we initially come to Christ, we are forgiven of our fleshly, sinful nature with its resultant past sins. (See Romans 3:24-25). God accepts and loves us as we are when we first come to Him. Amazingly, we have renewed fellowship with our Creator God through faith in Christ Jesus.

However, God loves us way too much to leave us in the condition we were in when we first came to Him! We have seen that the changes in us tend to occur gradually over time from "glory to glory." During these times of transition, the Lord shows great mercy to those whose hearts are set on obedience to Him while they struggle with their flesh to overcome sin in their lives. We serve a merciful God who also looks at the intention of our heart! (See 1 Samuel 16:7.)

~

Psalm 103:12 - "As far as the east is from the west, so far hath He removed our transgressions from us."

Hebrews 10:17 - "And their sins and iniquity I will remember no more."

Imagine this, once we have been forgiven of sins of which we have repented, the Lord promises that He will remember them no more! It's over, done, and forgotten. Now, it is our job to align our thoughts with the thoughts of God, and forgive ourselves, and move on in our walk with the Lord. The best is yet to come!

~

Having accepted Christ Jesus as my Lord and Savior, I can confidently say out loud:

"I am… redeemed and forgiven!"

NOTES ON:
I AM... REDEEMED AND FORGIVEN!

NOTES ON:
I AM... REDEEMED AND FORGIVEN!

CHAPTER 4
I AM... NO LONGER A SLAVE TO SIN

> Romans 6:6-7 - "Knowing this, that our old man is crucified with Him, that the body of sin might be destroyed, that henceforth we should not serve sin. For he that is dead is freed from sin."

As we have seen previously, when we are filled with the Holy Spirit of the living God, those bondages or chains that keep us entangled in sin are broken such that we are no longer a slave to sin. This does not mean that we are miraculously delivered from a particular sin in an instant, although it certainly can and has happened in this manner for some. Typically, the outward manifestation of no longer participating in a particular sin occurs over time as we work cooperatively with the promptings of the Holy Spirit who now lives within us.

The Holy Spirit will be quick to convict us of sin in our lives. The new, soft heart in a believer will feel remorse at this conviction and strive to no longer participate in that sin. When our heart, mind, will, and emotions are aligned with the heart, mind, will, and emotions of God, it will only be a matter of time before that sin becomes a distant memory for us. Remember, God sees the end from the beginning. Our job is to trust God, have faith in Him and His promises, and cooperate with the work of the Holy Spirit who lives within us.

And yes, overcoming sin can be an enormous struggle for some of us. I don't mean to minimize the struggle. I wrote about this in my book, *Ready for the King:*[2]

> Some might ask "Why does a loving God allow the struggle?" The answer may lie in the story of how a mere caterpillar transforms into a beautiful butterfly. As you know, the caterpillar wraps itself tightly in a cocoon, much like our more serious challenges here on earth can bind us up also. Once the caterpillar has

_____

[2] *Ready for the King, A Journey to the Heart of Jesus to Prepare for His Return* © 2023, Manifest Publications

changed into a butterfly, it has to free itself from the cocoon. This newly formed butterfly is stuffed in this strong cocoon barely able to move, let alone fight its way out with a newly formed and unfamiliar body.

Those of us with "softer hearts" may want so much to help that baby butterfly! However, what would happen if we came along, interrupted God's perfect plan for that butterfly, and carefully cracked open that tough cocoon to free that butterfly from that tough situation? Do you realize that the butterfly would not be able to fly and would soon die? In fact, it is that difficult struggle to free itself from the cocoon that builds its muscles and makes it strong enough to fly and become what God always intended for it to be!

Similarly, our struggles with sin in this life serve to strengthen our spiritual muscles so to speak. Our struggles can also strengthen our resolve to submit to the Holy Spirit and strengthen our faith and trust in God. Once we emerge victorious over sin through faith in, reliance on, and obedience to Christ, it places us in a new position to teach and encourage others who struggle in a similar manner. God never wastes our pain or lessons learned in the struggle. Since God will never give up on us (see Isaiah 41:10), we need to align our thoughts with His and never give up on ourselves either.

~

Romans 8:2 - "For the law of the Spirit of life in Christ Jesus hath made me free from the law of sin and death."

Romans 6:16-18 - "Know ye not, that to whom ye yield yourselves servants to obey, his servant ye are to whom ye obey; whether of sin unto death, or of obedience unto righteousness? But God be thanked, that ye were the servants of sin, but ye have obeyed from the heart that form of doctrine which was delivered you. Being them made free from sin, ye became the servants of righteousness."

Romans 6:22 - "But now being made free from sin, you become

> servants to God, ye have your fruit
> unto holiness, and the end
> everlasting life.

These scriptures state the truth of our being set free from the bondage of sin once we come to faith in Christ Jesus and make Him our LORD. In Matthew 6:24, we read that no one can serve two masters. We must **choose** whom we will serve. We can serve our sinful self, or we can choose to serve a righteous God. This is a choice each one of us must make, and no choice is a choice. Remember, each choice results in a different eternal destination. When we choose self in this earthly life, our eternity will be spent in eternal torment separated from our Creator God; while choosing God through faith in His only begotten Son, Christ Jesus, in this earthly life will result in a wonderful eternity spent in the presence of our Creator God. It truly is just that simple!

~

> John 8:36 - [Jesus speaking] "If the
> Son therefore shall make you free,
> ye shall be free indeed."

Our job is **only** to trust, believe, and obey the promptings of the Holy Spirit. Should we fail along the way as we often do, we are to repent, accept God's forgiveness, dust ourselves off, and try again. Please remember that part of accepting God's forgiveness involves aligning our thoughts with His, even forgiving ourselves! The bible is a book of victory, not defeat!

~

Having accepted Christ Jesus as my Lord and Savior, I can confidently say out loud:

"I have… been set free from sin!"

NOTES ON:
I AM... NO LONGER A SLAVE OF SIN!

NOTES ON:

I AM... NO LONGER A SLAVE OF SIN!

CHAPTER 5
I HAVE... ETERNAL LIFE WITH GOD

John 3:16 – [Jesus speaking] For God so loved the world, that he gave his only begotten Son, that whosoever believeth in him should not perish, but have everlasting life.

There is no better scripture to begin this chapter than John 3:16! These words are a promise given directly by the Lord Himself!

There are also several other scriptures which confirm that those who are in Christ are promised eternal life in the presence of the Lord.

~

Romans 6:23 - "For the wages of sin is death; but the gift of God is eternal life through Jesus Christ our Lord."

We can either choose to serve sin and suffer by having to pay the cost of this choice, which is the second death in eternal torment separated from God; or we can receive the most precious gift of eternal life when we choose to serve God. The choice we make in this lifetime truly does determine our eternal destination. It really is just that simple. We must make a choice, and these choices can be summarized as follows:

"Two masters: sin and God

Two methods: wages and free gift.

Two aftermaths: death and eternal life."[3]

We must choose!

~

John 10:27-28 - [Christ Jesus speaking] "My sheep hear My voice, and I know them, and they follow Me: and I give unto them eternal life; and they shall never perish, neither shall any man pluck

---

[3] Quote from p 1699 in Believer's Bible Commentary, 2nd Edition

them out of my Father's hand."

In this passage, Christ Jesus speaks of some of the qualities demonstrated in the lives of those on earth who are His and have eternal life. In other words, those who have a saving faith. These are those who believe in, have faith in, follow, and obey Christ Jesus. Born-again believers not only follow Christ Jesus like sheep follow their shepherd, but are promised that there is nothing in all creation that can forcibly remove them from God against their will. (See Romans 8:38-39.) We are protected in this promise in the words of our Lord and Savior Himself!

~

1 Timothy 6:12 - "Fight the good fight of faith, lay hold on eternal life, whereunto thou art also called, and hast professed a good profession before many witnesses."

This verse in 1 Timothy illustrates some character-istics of a born-again believer who is promised eternal life. It boils down to a steadfast faith in Christ Jesus and His redemptive work on the cross. It is our faith alone in Christ Jesus that saves us. Our saving faith is manifested to others because it results in a walk of obedience to

Christ Jesus for the remainder of our natural lives on this earth. Paul is comparing our resultant walk with Christ Jesus as a marathon when he speaks of "fighting the good fight of faith." Our obedience to God is the result of our love for and saving faith in Christ Jesus.

~

Galatians 6:8 - "For he that soweth to his flesh shall of the flesh reap corruption; but he that soweth to the Spirit shall of the Spirit reap life everlasting."

This verse illustrates that we will reap what we sow. The definition of corruption in this instance is the act of being in a state of moral depravity or sinfulness. When we serve our flesh, we remain in a state of sinfulness. We have already seen that God will not dwell with sin. When we are born again, we are filled with the Holy Spirit of the living God and the righteousness of Christ Jesus is imputed to us. Once we are undeservedly seen as righteous, we can dwell in the presence of God in restored fellowship with Him and experience the promise of eternal life with Him. The choices we make on this earth truly do determine our eternal destination.

~

1John 2:17 - "And the world passeth away, and the lust thereof: but he that doeth the will of God abideth for ever."

1 John 5:13 - "These things have I written unto you that believe on the name of the Son of God; that ye may know that ye have eternal life, and that ye may believe on the name of the Son of God."

Again, eternal life with God is promised to those who are in Christ Jesus! Those who have a saving faith in Christ Jesus will manifest it through their obedience to the Word of God in their lives.

~

Having accepted Christ Jesus as my Lord and Savior, I can confidently say out loud:

"I have... eternal life in Christ!"

NOTES ON:
I HAVE... ETERNAL LIFE IN CHRIST!

NOTES ON:
I HAVE... ETERNAL LIFE IN CHRIST!

NOTES ON:
I HAVE... ETERNAL LIFE IN CHRIST!

CHAPTER 6
I WAS... CREATED WITH A PURPOSE

Imagine that! Each and every one of us was created by almighty God with a specific purpose in mind! God chose to create **you** with specific attributes, in specific life circumstances, connected to specific people, at a specific time in human history, for a specific kingdom purpose. **You** are important to God and His kingdom purposes!

~

> *Ephesians 1:4-5 - "According as He hath chosen us in Him before the foundation of the world, that we should be holy and without blame before Him in love: having predestinated us unto the adoption of children by Jesus Christ to*

*Himself, according to the good
pleasure of His will."*

This verse clearly expresses the fact that God
chose each and every one of us before He
even began the actual process of creation. He
knew each of us individually and desired for
each of us to become a child of the Father
through faith in Christ Jesus. His desire was and
is that each of us would choose to live holy lives
on this earth out of our love for Him. God desired
you and intentionally formed you! Regardless of
what anyone says or what you might think, you
were **not** an accident!

~

*Ephesians 2:10 - "For we are His
workmanship, created in Christ
Jesus unto good works, which
God hath before ordained that
we should walk in them."*

We are the workmanship of God on two levels.
First, we were intentionally created in the physical
realm by God for His good pleasure and for a
purpose. Secondly, when we are filled with the
Holy Spirit and born again spiritually, we become
a child of the living God and a member of the
family of God through God's design, workmanship, and divine plan. Although we are not saved
by good works, we were created **for** good works.

Our good works are the result of our saving faith, and the purpose for which we were created.

And, we must remember, the exact nature of the God-ordained good works is different and specific for each and every one of us. I like to envision a huge puzzle with billions of pieces of which no two are the same. Each piece is equally important in order for God's overall kingdom plan to be achieved. Yes, you are very important to God and His kingdom purposes. There is only one you!

~

Psalms 139: 13-16 - "For thou hast possessed my reins; thou hast covered me in my mother's womb. I will praise thee; for I am fearfully and wonderfully made: marvellous are thy works; and that my soul knoweth right well. My substance was not hid from thee, when I was made in secret, and curiously wrought in the lowest parts of the earth. Thine eyes did see my substance, yet being unperfect; and in thy book all my members were written, which were in continuance fashioned, when as yet there was none of them."

The miraculous formation of a new human being is truly beyond our comprehension. Only an omnipotent God could place **all** of our attributes into a microscopic singular cell, formed partially from the mother and partially from the father, that will divide and eventually turn into a new and unique human being. Consider that from this singular microscopic cell, the following will develop: " 60 trillion cells, 100 thousand miles of nerve fiber, 60 thousand miles of vessels carrying blood around the body, 250 bones, to say nothing of the joints, ligaments, and muscles."[4] It is truly mind boggling when you consider the billions upon billions of individually unique people formed in the past, in the present, as well as those who will be formed in the future! And just think, each one of us was intentionally formed in this manner for God's kingdom purpose. God is truly amazing!

~

> *Jeremiah 1:5 - "Before I formed thee in the belly I knew thee; and before thou camest out of the womb I sanctified thee, and I ordained thee a prophet unto the nations."*

This was the word of God spoken to the prophet

─────────────────────────

[4] Quote from p 704 of Believer's Bible Commentary, 2nd Edition

Jeremiah. He was directly told by God that he was known by God before he was even born, and that he was sanctified or, by definition, set aside for God's specific purpose of being a prophet to the nations. Since God is no respecter of persons, each of us was also known by God before we were born and set aside for the purposes of God. Although not everyone is called to be a prophet, we each do have a specific and important purpose in God.

~

> Colossians 1:16 - "For by Him were all things created, that are in heaven, and that are in earth, visible and invisible, whether they be thrones, or dominions, or principalities, or powers: all things were created by Him and for Him."

Again, the Lord created absolutely everything in the universe with intention, and everything was created **for** Him and His purposes!

~

Having accepted Christ Jesus as my Lord and Savior, I can confidently say out loud:

"I was... uniquely created with intention for a special purpose of God!"

NOTES ON:
I WAS... CREATED WITH A PURPOSE!

NOTES ON:
I WAS... CREATED WITH A PURPOSE!

NOTES ON:
I WAS... CREATED WITH A PURPOSE!

CHAPTER 7
I AM... CHOSEN

> *1 Peter 2:9-10 - "But ye are a chosen generation, a royal priesthood, an holy nation, a peculiar people; that ye should shew forth the praises of Him who hath called you out of darkness into His marvelous light: which in time past were not a people, but are now the people of God: which had not obtained mercy, but now have obtained mercy."*

Under the old covenant, Israel alone was God's chosen people from the time of Abraham until the coming of Messiah Jesus. During the exodus when Moses was leading the Israelites out of Egypt into the promised land, God gave a directive to Moses to share with the Israelites that if they would obey Him and keep His covenant, God would treasure the chosen Jewish people above all the people of the earth and make them a holy nation. (See Exodus 19:5-6.) However, due to the disobedience and unbelief of the Jewish people, the nation of Israel failed as God's chosen people to bring His salvation to all the nations and therefore, forfeited their initial position. Today under the new covenant, it is believers in Christ Jesus, whether Jew or Gentile, who are God's chosen people with the given task of shining the light of His salvation to every nation, tribe, and tongue.

Everyone who is currently a believer was once in darkness and enslaved to sin before they came to faith in Christ Jesus. But the Lord God through His infinite mercy has offered salvation to **all** of His human creation through faith in His only begotten Son. Jewish people who have come to faith in Christ Jesus have been restored to fellowship with God, and Gentiles (non-Jewish people) who have come to faith in Christ Jesus are included in this great gift of salvation. Please remember, God still remembers and loves His Israel and will call them to Himself after the fullness of the Gentiles has come in. (See Romans 11:25.)

~

John 15:16 – [Jesus speaking] "Ye have not chosen me, but I have chosen you, and ordained you, that ye should go and bring forth fruit, and that your fruit should remain: that whatsoever ye shall ask of the Father in My name, He may give it you."

Matthew 28:19-20 - Go ye therefore, and teach all nations, baptizing them in the name of the Father, and of the Son, and of the Holy Ghost: Teaching them to observe all things whatsoever I have commanded you: and, lo, I am with you alway, [even] unto the end of the world. Amen.

In John 15, Jesus is speaking to His original twelve apostles about bearing fruit for His Kingdom. Matthew 28 is the "great commission" to spread the good news of the Gospel and bring souls to salvation through faith in Jesus Christ. Jesus was appointing them into ministry for His Kingdom. Perhaps, having human flaws, the apostles needed a reminder that they were intentionally chosen by God for a specific God-ordained purpose and needed to hear the promise that power from on high would be provided to them so they could accomplish this task and fulfill the mission.

We must ask if we are any different than the original apostles? Obviously, we have not walked and talked with Christ Jesus in human form upon this earth as the original apostles did. However, **all** those who come to Christ are appointed to the great commission of bringing people to Christ for their eternal salvation and making more disciples. God's main goal is that He would have it that none be lost and that everyone is given an opportunity to choose Him for their eternal salvation.

~

Ephesians 1:4 - "According as He hath chosen us in Him before the foundation of the world, that we should be holy and without blame before Him in love:"

Before God created the universe and everything in it, He chose to make human beings in His image. (See Genesis 1:26.) God intentionally chose and planned to create each human being for the purpose of living holy and consecrated lives unto Him out of our love for Him. However, He also gave man free will to choose God's way of living or not. God prefers that we would choose to live our lives His way unto eternal salvation, but He will not force us to do it His way. Our rejection of God's way will lead to eternal damnation. The choice is ours to make during our lives upon the earth, but the consequence of our choice is eternal. Whatever choice we make does not change the fact that each of us was specifically created and called by God for His purposes!

~

> 2 Thessalonians 2:13 - "But we are bound to give thanks always to God for you, brethren beloved of the Lord, because God hath from the beginning chosen you to salvation through sanctification of the Spirit and belief of the truth:"

In this scripture, Paul tells the Thessalonian Christians that God chose each of them unto salvation before the dawn of time. Although God's plan of salvation is available to every person He created, it can only be received by God's grace through faith in His only begotten Son, Jesus Christ. 2 Peter 3:9 makes clear that it is not God's desire for any to perish. But He never takes away our free will to make that choice accordingly. It is God's desire that you choose Him!

~

Having accepted Christ Jesus as my Lord and Savior, I can confidently say out loud:

"I am… God's chosen!"

NOTES ON:
I AM... GOD'S CHOSEN!

Notes on:
I am... God's chosen!

CHAPTER 8
I HAVE... PEACE IN CHRIST

Philippians 4:6-7 - "Be careful for nothing; but in everything by prayer and supplication with thanksgiving let your requests be known unto God. And the peace of God, which passeth all understanding, shall keep your hearts and minds through Christ Jesus."

This verse is telling followers of Christ not to be anxious about anything. Our level of anxiousness never affects the outcome of a situation and is, therefore, unnecessary. Instead, we are to continuously pray to God, making our needs and wants known to Him, while trusting that He alone is our source for help and knows what is best for each and every one of us. Our prayers to God should be done with thanksgiving for all He has already done for us and how He has proved His steadfastness and trustworthiness over and over again in our lives.

Our hearts contain our passions, while our minds contain our understanding and conscience. When the Holy Spirit resides within us and we submit to Him, He maintains a sense of peace within our heart and mind even during the tribulations of life. We know through scripture that only God can take something meant for our harm and work it out for good in our lives. (See Romans 8:28.) We also know that God only has plans to prosper us and not to harm us. (See Jeremiah 29:11.) Because of these promises of God, we can truly have a peace that surpasses all understanding in the midst of the storms of life. This can only be achieved when one is in relationship with the living God!

~

> *Romans 15:13 - "Now the God of hope fill you with all joy and peace in believing, that ye may abound in hope, through the power of the Holy Ghost."*

By grace through faith in Christ Jesus, both Jewish and Gentile believers have the hope of eternal life spent with the Lord. The Holy Spirit within us not only gives believers steadfast peace and joy in the assurance of eternal life spent with God, but the peace and joy of knowing we are traveling in this earthly life with God's presence residing within us! Hebrews 13:5 tells us that God will never leave us nor forsake us! This should be a great comfort to all believers in Christ Jesus no matter what we are experiencing on this earth.

~

> *Romans 5:1 - "Therefore being justified by faith, we have peace with God through our Lord Jesus Christ:"*

Prior to coming to faith in Christ Jesus, each and every one of us was separated from a holy God due to sin. Our fleshly nature is in opposition to, or enmity with, God. When we come to faith in Christ Jesus, we are reconciled back to a holy God only by His grace. The Holy Spirit who now dwells within us as born-again believers is the seal that we have been reconnected back to God and are now at peace with Him.

~

> *John 14:27 - [Jesus speaking]*

"Peace I leave with you, my peace I give unto you: not as the world giveth, give I unto you. Let not your heart be troubled, neither let it be afraid."

The Lord is now bequeathing His peace unto His followers. His peace is a true tranquility of the soul, consistent contentment of mind, and everlasting relationship with the Father in heaven just as Christ Jesus had and has. The world gives empty wishes of peace which it cannot guarantee. Conversely, Jesus is the prince, author, promoter, and keeper of the peace. Only Christ Jesus can offer the guarantee of inner peace when we follow Him.

The Lord ends this verse by telling His followers not to fear the evil soon to come. The evil to which He is referring is His death by crucifixion. This evil was to fall upon the Lord only, but the result would be good: the salvation and redemption to all those in an otherwise lost world.

~

Isaiah 26:3 - "Thou wilt keep him in perfect peace, whose mind is stayed on thee: because he trusteth in Thee."

70

Those who trust in the Lord and keep their minds fixed on Him are promised perfect peace in this world as well as the next. We can rest assured that the Lord will keep all of His promises to His followers.

~

Having accepted Christ Jesus as my Lord and Savior, I can confidently say out loud:

"I have… peace in Christ Jesus!"

NOTES ON:
I HAVE... PEACE IN CHRIST JESUS!

NOTES ON:
I HAVE... PEACE IN CHRIST JESUS!

NOTES ON:
I HAVE... PEACE IN CHRIST JESUS!

CHAPTER 9
I HAVE... VICTORY IN CHRIST

Philippians 4:13 - "I can do all things through Christ which strengtheneth me."

This is an interesting verse, often taken out of context to mean that the Holy Spirit will give me the strength to accomplish whatever I want to accomplish whenever I want to accomplish it. This is **not** what this verse means.

This verse is telling us that because the Holy Spirit now lives within us, we now have the strength required to endure to the end. We now can live lives of faith in obedience to the word of God for the remainder of our time upon this earth. We now have the strength to overcome sin in our lives. We now have the strength to accomplish the kingdom purpose tasks for which each one of us was individually and intentionally created. We now have the strength to maintain our inner peace during the storms of life. We could not do any of these things while we are/were in the flesh without the support of the Holy Spirit within us. The provision and working of the Holy Spirit within us is how the Lord shows His strength through our weaknesses. (See 2 Corinthians 12:9.)

~

> *2 Timothy 1:7 - "For God hath not given us a spirit of fear; but of power, and of love, and of a sound mind."*

After the exodus from Egypt when Moses climbed Mount Sinai, God gave Moses His laws with much lightning and thunderings which, naturally, frightened Moses as well as the Israelites. In contrast, Christ Jesus who was the Word of God made flesh, taught the principles of God in love and humility in an inviting fashion while He walked upon this earth. Christ's method of teaching did not invoke fear but, rather, invoked love. Christ displayed true and perfect humility, which is strength and power under control.

When the Holy Spirit resides within us, we can submit willingly to His promptings, with trust in the assurance that the basis of the promptings will always be good. The Lord's message was all about love and justice. Because of that, we have no need to fear. The Holy Spirit gives us the power to live in submissive obedience to the word of God and the promptings of the Holy Spirit. As part of the Lord's directives, our love of the Lord and love for our fellow man will prompt us to do the good works of the Spirit. Finally, when our thoughts and heart are aligned with the thoughts and heart of God, we will have a sound, peaceful mind.

~

> Romans 8:37 - "Nay, in all these things we are more than conquerors through Him that loved us."

Paul was stating that, although Christians were suffering much persecution for their faithfulness to the gospel message of Christ, we could all rest assured in the promises of Christ. The promises to which he was referring was our ultimate triumph over the bondages of sin with its resultant second death in eternal torment. Faithful followers of Christ Jesus are promised eternal life spent with the Lord!

~

1 John 4:4 - "Ye are of God, little children, and have overcome them: because greater is He that is in you, than he that is in the world."

This is one of my favorite verses of scripture. Prior to coming to faith in Christ, we are nothing more than slaves to sin under the rule of Satan in this world. Once we come to faith in Christ and accept Jesus as our Lord and Savior, we are then filled with the Holy Spirit of the living God! There is nothing in the universe that is more powerful than our God. Even Satan, as the temporary ruler of this world, has constraints placed upon him by our almighty God.

And remember this, our bodies are the temple, or dwelling place, of the Holy Spirit of God! This is an amazing truth that, "greater is He that is in us than he that is in the world," and "if God be for us, who can be against us? (See 1 John 4:4; Romans 8:31.) When we are filled with the Holy Spirit and are functioning within God's will for our lives, we have direct access to the unlimited love, power, and protection of almighty God! You cannot beat that!

~

> *1 Corinthians 15:57 - "But thanks be to God, which giveth us the victory through our Lord Jesus Christ."*

Simply stated, born-again believers in Christ have the full assurance of victory over sin, Satan, death, and hell when we live upon this earth in obedience to the word of God and the promptings of the Holy Spirit. We came from God in eternity, and born-again believers in Christ Jesus are promised to return to our original home in eternity with God after our earthly lives are finished. Now that is true victory!

~

Having accepted Christ Jesus as my Lord and Savior, I can confidently say out loud:

"I have... victory in Christ!"

NOTES ON:
I HAVE... VICTORY IN CHRIST!

NOTES ON:
I HAVE... VICTORY IN CHRIST!

NOTES ON:
I HAVE... VICTORY IN CHRIST!

CHAPTER 10
I AM... NOT ALONE

*John 14:16-18 - [Jesus speaking]
"And I will pray the father, and He
shall give you another Comforter,
that He may abide with you for
ever; Even the Spirit of truth; whom
the world cannot receive, because
it seeth Him not, neither knoweth
Him: but ye know Him; for He
dwelleth with you, and shall be in
you. I will not leave you comfortless:
I will come to you."*

*1 Corinthians 3:16 - "Know ye not
that ye are the temple of God,
and that the Spirit of God dwelleth
in you?*

Because Christ Jesus was the ultimate and final sacrifice required by the Father for the forgiveness of the sin of man, Jesus became the only mediator through which we can have reconciliation back to the Father. After His resurrection from the dead but prior to Jesus leaving this world to ascend and return to the Father, He promised His followers that another comforter would be sent unto them.

The word for comforter used in the original text is *paracletos* and has a much richer meaning than just comforter. It also means defender, advocate, counsellor, teacher, and mediator. This is the function of the Holy Spirit of the living God. When we come to faith in Christ by the grace of God, He sends His Holy Spirit to each and every one of us to live within us. This is what it means to be born again. When we are born again, we carry the Holy Spirit of the living God within us wherever we go twenty-four hours a day, 365 days per year. We are truly never alone!

~

> *Matthew 28:20 – [Jesus speaking before His ascension] "Teaching them to observe all things whatsoever I have commanded you: and, Lo, I am with you alway, even unto the end of the world."*

In this passage, Jesus is assuring His followers that He will always be with them until the end of this world. We have just read that this is accomplished through the infilling of the Holy Spirit in born-again believers.

~

> *Hebrews 13:5-6 - "Let your conversation be without covetousness; and be content with such things as ye have: for He hath said, I will never leave thee, nor forsake thee. So that we may boldly say, the Lord is my helper, and I will not fear what man shall do unto me."*

In these verses, the author (most likely the apostle Paul or one of his associates) is writing to the believing Jews who are suffering much persecution. The author is warning the converted Jews to be content with what they have and to not be covetous of what they no longer had. He comforts them by reminding them that God will never leave them as orphans or forsake them because He has sent the comforter, or Holy Spirit, to dwell within each of them individually. Just a few verses later, it is made clear that the Lord is the same yesterday, today, and forever! (See Hebrews 13:8.) This means that we can rest assured that He will never leave nor forsake us either!

~

Isaiah 41:10,13 - "Fear thou not; for I am with thee: be not dismayed; for I Am thy God: I will strengthen thee; yea, I will help thee; yea, I will uphold thee with the right hand of my righteousness. For I the Lord thy God will hold thy right hand, saying unto thee, Fear not; I will help thee."

In this passage of scripture, the prophet Isaiah is prophesying to the Israelites of the promise of their impending release from captivity under the Babylonians which the mighty hand of the God of Abraham, Isaac, and Jacob would accomplish for them. Those of us today can look back into history and see how God kept all of the promises He made to His chosen people of Israel. Our God really is faithful and true!

~

Joshua 1:9 - "Have I not commanded thee? Be strong and of a good courage; be not afraid, neither be thou dismayed: for the

Lord thy God is with thee whither-soever thou goest."

Joshua was charged by God to lead the Israelites to the promised land after the death of Moses. God assured Joshua of victory over all enemies who would try to thwart the Israelites from entering their promised land. God, Himself, promised to be with Joshua wherever he went and therefore, there would be no reason for him to fear or become discouraged. How much more so does this apply to the born-again followers of Christ under the new covenant who carry the Holy Spirit of the living God within them!?!

~

Having accepted Christ Jesus as my Lord and Savior, I can confidently say out loud:

"I am... never alone!"

NOTES ON:
I AM... NEVER ALONE!

NOTES ON:
I AM... NEVER ALONE!

NOTES ON:
I AM... NEVER ALONE!

CHAPTER 11
SUMMARY

No matter what you are experiencing in this natural life or even what your belief systems are at this present moment in time, rest assured that you are loved by the living and almighty God of Abraham, Isaac, and Jacob! You can say with full confidence that "I am loved by God, the creator of the universe!" Yes, it is true that God loves you just the way you are. And, it is also true that God loves you way too much to leave you as He found you once you are reconciled back to Him!

God sent His only begotten Son, Jesus Christ, to this earth to be the propitiation, or payment, necessary for the forgiveness of the sins of man. Since our sin separates us from a Holy God, we must be forgiven of our sins in order to be reconciled back to our holy God. This reconciliation back to God can only happen when we accept the sacrifice of Christ Jesus on the cross and follow Him. Christ Jesus is the only mediator between sinful man and God. We can only be reconciled back to God and saved by the grace of God through faith in His only begotten Son, Christ Jesus.

When we are saved by grace through faith, the Holy Spirit of the living God takes up residence inside of us. How amazing is this?! But what is even more amazing is that there are so many other things which become true about us when the Holy Spirit lives within us! Once saved, we can now say the following with full confidence:

- I am not only loved but I am a new creature in Christ,
- I am a child of the living God, I am forgiven and redeemed,
- I am no longer a slave to sin,
- I have eternal life with God,
- I was intentionally made with a purpose,
- I am chosen,
- I have peace in Christ,
- I have victory in Christ,
- and I am never alone!

When we first come to Christ and are saved, most often our life in the natural still looks and feels the same as it always was. Those around us cannot yet see the promised changes within us. But, rest assured, when you remain steadfast in your new faith, which should always be growing, those changes **will** manifest themselves in time! Remember, God can see the end from the beginning, thus making all these promised changes in us true from the moment we accept Christ Jesus as our Lord and Savior.

I would also like to add Deuteronomy 28:13 to this summary because it states, "And the Lord God shall make thee the head, and not the tail; and thou shalt be above only, and thou shalt not be beneath; if that thou harken unto the commandments of the Lord thy God, which I command thee this day, to observe and to do them:" God promises to do His part when we do our part, which is to love Him, have faith in Him, trust in Him, and obey Him!

And now, I close this book with the priestly blessing upon your life. It is truly my heart's desire to see you blessed by God through your faith in Christ Jesus and the fulfillment of all of His promises to you.

Numbers 6:24-26 - The Lord bless thee and keep thee: The Lord make His face shine upon thee, and be gracious to thee: the Lord lift up His countenance upon thee, and give thee peace."

Amen.

REFLECTIONS ABOUT MY IDENTITY IN CHRIST:

REFLECTIONS ABOUT MY IDENTITY IN CHRIST:

REFLECTIONS ABOUT MY IDENTITY IN CHRIST:

ABOUT THE AUTHOR

For as long as she can remember, Catherine Vitetta always loved her Lord and Savior, Jesus. Catherine and her husband, George, had a home church with multiple small community outreaches until George went to be with the Lord in 2022. Now, she is going even deeper in her relationship with the Lord by serving Him in new and unexpected ways, including writing books! It is Catherine's desire that this book will draw each reader into a better understanding of who we are in Christ, and into a more intimate relationship with Jesus so that you can experience the same love, peace, and joy that she has found in Him!

ABOUT MANIFEST PUBLICATIONS

Manifest Publications is the publishing division of Manifest International, LLC. Our objective is to help like-minded ministries and writers produce and distribute materials which proclaim Jesus Christ to all the world and equip the global Church for unity and maturity.

MANIFEST
PUBLICATIONS

www.manifestinternational.com

www.ingramcontent.com/pod-product-compliance
Lightning Source LLC
LaVergne TN
LVHW021405080426
835508LV00020B/2463